# CAMBRIDGE LIBRARY COLLECTION

*Books of enduring scholarly value*

## Women's Writing

The later twentieth century saw a huge wave of academic interest in women's writing, which led to the rediscovery of neglected works from a wide range of genres, periods and languages. Many books that were immensely popular and influential in their own day are now studied again, both for their own sake and for what they reveal about the social, political and cultural conditions of their time. A pioneering resource in this area is Orlando: Women's Writing in the British Isles from the Beginnings to the Present (http://orlando.cambridge.org), which provides entries on authors' lives and writing careers, contextual material, timelines, sets of internal links, and bibliographies. Its editors have made a major contribution to the selection of the works reissued in this series within the Cambridge Library Collection, which focuses on non-fiction publications by women on a wide range of subjects from astronomy to biography, music to political economy, and education to prison reform.

## Reflections upon the Education of Children in Charity Schools

Sarah Trimmer was an experienced Sunday and charity school educator, remembered for her popularization of images and fables in children's textbooks. Her ideas were already well respected during her lifetime and many of her books saw multiple editions, eliciting the interest of such figures as Queen Charlotte and the Dowager Countess Spencer. Her *Reflections upon the Education of Children in Charity Schools*, first published in 1792, was one of several books she wrote to advise her readers on how to approach the Christian education of the poor. In it, Trimmer passionately advocated the utility of charity schools, provided that they followed a more age-appropriate and critical curriculum, which she conveniently published as separate editions. Those interested in the history of education, social history, the Society for the Propagation of Christian Knowledge, or the changing voice of female authorship will benefit from this book. For more information on this author, see http://orlando.cambridge.org/public/svPeople?person_id=trimsa

Cambridge University Press has long been a pioneer in the reissuing of out-of-print titles from its own backlist, producing digital reprints of books that are still sought after by scholars and students but could not be reprinted economically using traditional technology. The Cambridge Library Collection extends this activity to a wider range of books which are still of importance to researchers and professionals, either for the source material they contain, or as landmarks in the history of their academic discipline.

Drawing from the world-renowned collections in the Cambridge University Library, and guided by the advice of experts in each subject area, Cambridge University Press is using state-of-the-art scanning machines in its own Printing House to capture the content of each book selected for inclusion. The files are processed to give a consistently clear, crisp image, and the books finished to the high quality standard for which the Press is recognised around the world. The latest print-on-demand technology ensures that the books will remain available indefinitely, and that orders for single or multiple copies can quickly be supplied.

The Cambridge Library Collection will bring back to life books of enduring scholarly value (including out-of-copyright works originally issued by other publishers) across a wide range of disciplines in the humanities and social sciences and in science and technology.

# Reflections upon the Education of Children in Charity Schools

*With the Outlines of a Plan of Appropriate Instruction for the Children of the Poor*

Sarah Trimmer

CAMBRIDGE UNIVERSITY PRESS

Cambridge, New York, Melbourne, Madrid, Cape Town, Singapore,
São Paolo, Delhi, Dubai, Tokyo, Mexico City

Published in the United States of America by Cambridge University Press, New York

www.cambridge.org
Information on this title: www.cambridge.org/9781108018869



This edition first published 1792
This digitally printed version 2010

ISBN 978-1-108-01886-9 Paperback

# REFLECTIONS

UPON

THE EDUCATION OF CHILDREN

IN

# CHARITY SCHOOLS;

WITH

THE OUTLINES OF A PLAN OF APPROPRIATE INSTRUCTION

FOR

THE CHILDREN OF THE POOR;

SUBMITTED TO THE CONSIDERATION OF

*THE PATRONS*

OF SCHOOLS OF EVERY DENOMINATION, SUPPORTED BY CHARITY.

---

BY MRS. TRIMMER.

---

LONDON:
PRINTED FOR T. LONGMAN, PATERNOSTER-ROW; AND J. AND F. RIVINGTON, ST. PAUL'S CHURCH-YARD.

M.DCC.XCII.

# REFLECTIONS

UPON

THE EDUCATION OF CHILDREN

IN

*CHARITY SCHOOLS, &c.*

---

HAVING formed a plan for a courſe of inſtruction peculiarly adapted to the children of the poor, and prepared ſeveral articles of it for publication, I thought it incumbent upon me to explain my motives for an undertaking, which to ſome may appear ſuperfluous, and to others aſſuming, ſince the world already abounds with elementary books for Charity Schools, many of which were written by authors of the moſt eminent abilities, and higheſt reputation.

But firſt I ſhall beg leave to ſubmit to the conſideration of the benevolent a few hints which experience and obſervation have ſuggeſted to my mind, concerning thoſe inſtitutions which afford gratuitous inſtruction to the children of the poor, more particularly ſuch as are diſtinguiſhed from *Sunday*

*Schools* and *Schools of Induſtry*, by the name of CHARITY SCHOOLS.

The important queſtion, Whether it is conſiſtent with ſound policy to beſtow education upon children in the loweſt claſſes of life, has employed the pens of ſome of our beſt writers in the laſt and preſent centuries; and we may judge from the wonderful increaſe of ſchools ſupported by charitable contributions, that it is at length generally decided in the affirmative.

The objection againſt giving learning to the poor, leſt it raiſe them above their ſituation, is completely obviated by making ſuch learning as general as poſſible; for then it ceaſes to give pre-eminence, or to be a diſtinction, and muſt eventually qualify all better to fill their reſpective ſtations in ſociety: and nothing could be thought of ſo well calculated to diffuſe a moderate and uſeful ſhare of learning among the lower orders of people, as theſe ſchools. To this I may add, that as literature has made ſuch conſiderable advances in the kingdom, the poor ſeem to have a juſt claim to more liberal inſtruction than was formerly allotted to them. But there ſtill ſubſiſt various opinions in reſpect to the

the manner in which they ought to be educated, more particularly, whether the mode of *religious inſtruction* adopted at the firſt eſtabliſhed CHARITY SCHOOLS, in this kingdom, ſhould be continued in them, and extend to the inſtitutions of the preſent day; or whether charity children in general, but particularly thoſe trained in *Sunday Schools*, and *Day Schools of Induſtry*, ſhould not be taught upon a plan limited chiefly to leſſons of morality.

It is well known that thoſe uſeful eſtabliſhments, for which the nation is originally indebted to the wiſdom and piety of our anceſtors, and in which many thouſands of children are conſtantly training in habits of piety, virtue, and decorum, have owed their chief ſupport, from the beginning, to annual ſubſcriptions and voluntary benefactions, collected at the preaching of charity ſermons; we cannot therefore wonder that ſome of the truſtees and managers of Charity Schools, from zeal for their welfare, ſhould at firſt have viewed with a jealous eye the rapid progreſs of other inſtitutions for the inſtruction of poor children, from an apprehenſion that the ſucceſs of the one might interfere with the intereſts of the other, as they mutually depend on the ſame means for ſupport. But *Sunday Schools* and *Schools of Induſtry* have already exiſted long enough to prove that theſe fears were ill-grounded; for the beneficence of the preſent age is proportionate to its opulence, and every ſpecies of charity meets with ready contributors; ſo that there cannot be any real danger of the decay of *Charity Schools*, if they be properly conducted. Nothing can give *Sunday Schools* and *Schools of Induſtry* a preference to them, unleſs they afford better inſtruction.

It is much to be lamented, that inſtitutions reſpectively calculated, by their reflective and united benefits, to complete the long-deſired end, of educating all degrees of people in the lower ranks of life ſuitably to their various ſtations and callings, ſhould ever be regarded in the light of rivalſhip and competition. *Charity Schools* hold out ſuch ſuperior advantages, in ſome reſpects, as to give them a decided pre eminence over all the ſubſiſting eſtabliſhments for gratuitous inſtruction, as the money collected for them is uſually ſufficient to afford clothing to the children, as well as learning; and in many Charity Schools the children are entirely maintained in the houſe,

houſe, and ſome of them afterwards apprenticed to trades and manufactures.

But *Sunday Schools* and *Schools of Induſtry*, though the emoluments of the children are leſs, are of equal importance with the above inſtitutions, as they afford inſtruction to unlimited numbers of children, who could not be admitted into *Charity Schools*, on account of the expenſe attending them; neither could ſuch multitudes be trained up as *Charity Children* are, without great injury to ſociety: for, however deſirable it may be to reſcue the lower kinds of people from that deplorable ſtate of ignorance in which the greateſt part of them were for a long time ſuffered to remain, it cannot be right to train them *all* in a way which will moſt probably raiſe their ideas above the very loweſt occupations of life, and diſqualify them for thoſe ſervile offices which muſt be filled by ſome of the members of the community, and in which they may be equally happy with the higheſt, if they will do their duty.

Many ill conſequences are obſerved to ariſe among the higher orders of people from educating the children of perſons whoſe opulence is the fruit of their own induſtry, and who have

 made

made themſelves reſpectable without the aid of literary acquirements, together with thoſe whoſe parents are of high rank and independent fortune; but this injudicious practice we cannot expect to ſee aboliſhed while in the education of youth ſo much regard is paid to externals, and ſo little to the regulation of the heart and the improvement of the underſtanding. It will, however, readily be allowed, that the children of the poor ſhould not be educated in ſuch a manner as to ſet them above the occupations of humble life, or ſo as to make them uncomfortable among their equals, and ambitious of aſſociating with perſons moving in a higher ſphere, with whom they cannot poſſibly vie in expenſe or appearance without manifeſt injury to themſelves.

But there are degrees of poverty as well as of opulence; and if it be improper to educate the children of the higher claſſes promiſcuouſly, it ſurely muſt be equally ſo to place all the children of the poor upon the ſame footing, without any regard to the different circumſtances of their parents, or their own genius and capacity. It would be thought very cruel to ſend the child, or orphan, of a pious clergyman, or a reſpectable but reduced tradeſman, to be brought up among the offspring of thieves and vagabonds in the ſchools ſo happily and judiciouſly founded for thoſe moſt wretched of all poor children, by the Philanthropic Society; and it would appear very abſurd to ſend a boy deſigned for huſbandry to the Marine Society, to be educated in the art of navigation.

Yet nothing is more common than to mix poor children together in *Charity Schools*, whoſe ſeparate claims to the ſuperior advantages which theſe inſtitutions hold out, are by no means equal, and whoſe mental abilities will bear no compariſon.

It would be juſtly deemed very illiberal to refuſe to lads of bright parts, and uncommon activity of mind, the learning which *Charity Schools* afford, and conſign them to the labours of the field; but is it not equally injurious, both to ſociety and individuals, to condemn thoſe who are invincibly dull and ſtupid to literary ſtudies, as irkſome to them as the moſt ſervile occupations are to boys of quick parts and aſpiring tempers?

If there be among the poor children of a pariſh any who have been born to good proſpects, who have enjoyed in their earlieſt years the

the comforts of affluence, and who ſtill have reſpectable connections, it will be an act of particular kindneſs to place them in *Charity Schools*, where they will receive ſuch an education as may hereafter prove a means of reſtoring them to their former ſtation. And if there be others whoſe bright genius breaks through the thick clouds of ignorance and poverty, reaſon and humanity plead in their behalf, that they ſhould be indulged with ſuch tuition as may enable them to advance themſelves, by the exertion of their abilities, to a higher ſtation, and fill it with propriety. It certainly would be very unjuſtifiable to deny ſuch children a chance of bettering their condition.

For a conſiderable length of time it has been the uſual cuſtom to admit boys and girls into Charity Schools from the principle of lightening the burden of their parents, without any particular regard to their capacity for learning. Indeed, before the eſtabliſhment of Sunday Schools, there was no opportunity of giving them a probationary trial; but the happy period is at length arrived, which affords ſuitable inſtruction for poor children of all deſcriptions, for there

is

is ſcarcely an employment or condition in humble life to which there is not a ſchool adapted; the great difficulty ſeems to be, to form an accurate judgment of the objects for each particular charity, in order to make a proper ſelection of them.

In CHARITY SCHOOLS a comprehenſive plan of tuition holds forth advantages proper for the *firſt degree* among the lower orders, who in theſe ſeminaries might be qualified for teachers in ſchools ſupported by charity, for apprentices to common trades, and for domeſtic ſervants in reſpectable families.

DAY SCHOOLS OF INDUSTRY, by mixing labour with learning, are particularly eligible for ſuch children as are afterwards to be employed in manufactures, and other inferior offices in life, as well as for training thoſe who are uſually called *common ſervants*.

And SUNDAY SCHOOLS, while they hold out religious inſtruction ſuitable to all degrees of poor children, furniſh a ſufficient portion of learning* for ſuch as cannot be

* Excepting in the articles of writing and accounts, a little of which one could wiſh all the poor might obtain, though the ſabbath day is not the proper time for theſe acquirements.

ſpared

ſpared on week-days from the labours of the plough, or other occupations by which they contribute to the ſupport of families.

*Sunday Schools* may alſo ſerve (as was before hinted) as probationary ſchools to try the capacities of children previouſly to their admiſſion into *Charity Schools*.

Could this diſtribution of learning be univerſally made, I am perſuaded a very material objection to *Charity Schools* would be effectually done away: for by this means children endowed by nature with good capacities, would be put in the way to improve them; and others, to whom liberal inſtrüction would be no benefit, would be prevented from loſing that time over books which they might turn to more advantage by employing it in manual occupations.

It appears from the account of *Charity Schools* given by the *Society for the Propagation of Chriſtian Knowledge*, that there have been no leſs that 1631 of theſe ſchools eſtabliſhed in Great Britain ſince the reformation; in which, allowing for the deficiency occaſioned by ſome of them having been ſuffered to drop, there are ſtill 40,000 children educated annually.

At

At the firſt view we are ſurpriſed at the number of ſcholars in theſe ſchools; yet, when we conſider the multitudes of poor children there muſt neceſſarily be in ſuch a populous kingdom as this, it will appear comparatively ſmall: and it is proved to be actually ſo by the ſuperior numbers which already receive inſtruction in Sunday Schools, amounting, as I have been informed, to 500,000; and even this is greatly ſhort of the total number of poor children in the nation.

Day Schools of Induſtry have as yet made but little progreſs among us; but, from the happy ſucceſs of an experiment at this time making in one of the moſt populous pariſhes in London*, we may reaſonably hope to ſee, in the courſe of a few years, *Parochial Schools of Induſtry* in every pariſh of the metropolis, and in every town in England.

Till theſe Day Schools of Induſtry become

* The ſchool here alluded to is one eſtabliſhed about a year and a half ago, in the pariſh of Mary-le-bone, which is conducted on ſo excellent a plan, that it may properly ſerve as a pattern for other extenſive pariſhes in London. For arguments in favour of Parochial Schools of Induſtry, I ſhall refer my reader to a Pamphlet, written by Mr. Thomas Simons, one of the principal managers of the above ſchool. It is ſold by Meſſrs. Rivington, in St. Paul's Church-Yard.

a general

a general concern, they may be tried upon a ſmaller ſcale at an eaſy expenſe. I am happy in being able to mention one for girls in the ſame neighbourhood*, which is admirably conducted by a Society of Ladies.

In this little ſeminary the advantages of a *Charity School* and a *Day School of Induſtry* are united, for all the girls are taught to ſpin, knit, and work at their needles; they are alſo taught to read, nor is religious inſtruction omitted, and a few of them are maintained in the houſe, and inſtructed in every thing requiſite to qualify them for domeſtic ſervants. The annual ſubſcriptions toward this ſchool are in general half a guinea—the price of an *Opera Ticket*, as the benevolent foundreſs obſerved when ſhe propoſed its eſtabliſhment. Here may be frequently ſeen young ladies, accuſtomed to move in the firſt circles of elegance and faſhion, inſpecting the economy of this humble ſchool! Can a public entertainment, let the muſic be ever ſo enchanting, afford ſuch real, heart-felt ſatisfaction, as the exerciſe of benevolence like this neceſſarily produces?

If ſchools of this kind are found to ſucceed in the metropolis, there is a ſtill better

* No. 68, Edgware Road, near Portman Square.

chance for them in the country; and I have the happineſs of knowing ſeveral which are very beneficial to their reſpective neighbourhoods, by furniſhing well educated ſervants, particularly one at St. Alban's, under the patron ge and direction of a lady eminently diſtinguiſhed for zeal, activity, and judgment, in the exerciſe of the moſt diffuſive benevolence. This ſchool has the additional advantage of an excellent miſtreſs, who pays unremitting attention to the conduct of the children, and qualifies them for the various departments of domeſtic buſineſs, by attending to their ſeveral diſpoſitions and capacities—a diſtinction of more importance than it may at firſt appear.

In this ſchool Tables of Virtues and Vices are hung up in view, and each girl receives a ticket every night when her conduct in the day has been uniformly good; if any one has committed any of the faults enumerated in the Table of Vices, her ticket is withheld, and the offence marked in a book, which is occaſionally examined by the noble patroneſs, whoſe conſequent diſpleaſure, expreſſed in a mild reprimand, is uſually found a ſufficient puniſhment.

If

If Sunday Schools and Day Schools of Induſtry were univerſally eſtabliſhed, the education of the poor might be happily conducted; for then it would be no injury to them, upon the whole, to reduce conſiderably the number of ſcholars in *Charity Schools*, in order that the reſt might be maintained in the houſe, and kept apart from companions unſuitable to thoſe intended for what may be called the ſuperior ſtations of humble life, as well as from their own parents, many of whom, it is ſad to ſay! are but too apt to defeat the endeavours of thoſe who inſtruct their children, by encouraging them in goſſipping, tale-bearing, impertinence, and ingratitude; and very frequently by ſetting them examples of vice and profligacy.

This judicious meaſure of reducing the number of ſcholars for the purpoſes above mentioned, has been ſucceſsfully purſued by the truſtees of ſome of the *Charity Schools*; and the eſtabliſhment of *Parochial Day Schools*, ſhould it become general, will render it ſtill more practicable, becauſe the children who are excluded from the one, might be received by the other. But if *Charity Schools* cannot be put entirely upon this footing, they might ſurely be ſo contrived that all the children ſhould, in ſucceſſion, enjoy the benefit of this ſecluded education for the laſt year or two of their being at ſchool, in order to receive that *degree* of *religious inſtruction* which Charity Schools were originally deſigned to afford.

In founding theſe ſchools our pious anceſtors had evidently one great object in view, namely, to train the riſing generation of poor in the principles of the Reformed Religion, by making them thoroughly acquainted with the Holy Scriptures, and the Liturgy of the Eſtabliſhed Church. For the accompliſhment of this purpoſe they conceived a conſiderable portion of time would be requiſite. Under this idea, they thought proper to diſpenſe with *manual labour* in the early years of life, and, inſtead of contriving how to procure *work* for the children, they allotted them taſks of a *literary nature* only, that thoſe who were thus educated by the bounty of the public, might have full leiſure to purſue ſtudies of ſo much importance to their own eternal happineſs, and the intereſts of true Chriſtianity.

To promote ſtill farther their pious deſign of training the children of the poor in the knowledge and practice of religion and virtue, theſe truly Chriſtian patrons required that charity boys and girls ſhould be conducted to Church on Sundays, Wedneſdays, Fridays, and Holidays; and that they ſhould be frequently and publicly catechiſed by the miniſters of their reſpective pariſhes.

Whoever gives this plan attentive conſideration will find that it was, upon the whole, properly calculated to anſwer the purpoſes for which it was intended, and well ſuited to the times; and I ſubmit it to the determination of thoſe who are well-wiſhers to that religion which our forefathers were ſo zealous to eſtabliſh and propagate, whether it would not be better to continue to educate a *limited number* of boys and girls, with the ſame regard to the genuine principles of the Church of England, as one mean to prevent the ſpreading of thoſe erroneous doctrines which ſtrike at the very root of the Chriſtian Religion, inſtead of attempting to overturn the former ſyſtem, by making every *Charity School* a *Manufactory*.

Charity children thus educated might afterwards prove very inſtrumental to the propagation of true Chriſtianity. They would be eminently qualified for the office of ſchoolmaſters and miſtreſſes in the various deſcriptions of Charity Schools, which very few of the preſent generation fill with propriety. They would moſt likely make good apprentices, and conſcientious, faithful ſervants: ſuch ſervants as would deſerve to be preferred to the higheſt places in great families for their exemplary conduct; in which ſituations they would be able to continue the inſtruction of ſuch boys and girls from the Schools of Induſtry and Sunday Schools, as ſhould be placed under them in the loweſt offices of domeſtic ſervices; and, in caſe of matrimonial connection, they would be capable of teaching their own children; which would eventually leſſen the expenſe of *Sunday Schools* at leaſt, and, in a great meaſure, prove a ſubſtitute for them, if they ſhould unhappily fall into neglect.

I may farther add, that were the example of theſe perſons in proportion to their knowledge, it would operate greatly towards bringing about that reformation of manners which all who wiſh well to their country cannot but be anxious to ſee; and the advantages to thoſe young perſons who had been in *Sunday Schools* and *Schools of Induſtry*, would be inconceivably great were the upper ſervants capable and deſirous of contributing to their future improvement, inſtead of corrupting their minds by improper diſcourſe, and leading them aſtray by bad example; as is now too commonly the caſe.

It will be aſked, Is it neceſſary, in order for children to learn the principles of Chriſtianity, that they ſhould ſpend their whole time in literary acquirements and going to Church? By no means: for the common purpoſes of life a ſmall portion of time will ſuffice for the attainment of all that the poor have occaſion to know or practiſe; and even thoſe who are ſeparated from the multitude to receive a greater portion of learning, may have time to do many uſeful things beſides, as well as to recreate their minds by innocent amuſements, which are particularly requiſite for thoſe young people who have ſedentary employments *.

For

* It is, I believe, generally thought injudicious to excite an emulation in *Charity Boys* to write a fine hand; and, unleſs

For girls it is very eaſy to find intermediate employments; ſpinningwheels, both for wool and flax, ſhould be conſtant appendages to *Charity Schools,* not only upon the principle of economy, but for exerciſe, particularly the long running-wheel, which will be found very conducive to the health of thoſe children eſpecially who belong to the Cha-

unleſs they are intended for teachers in ſchools, this certainly had better be avoided; neither ſhould any but theſe be encouraged to make a proficiency in figures beyond what may be wanted for apprentices to common trades. The generality of charity boys may be more advantageouſly occupied in helping to teach the younger ones, and in committing different things to memory; and I cannot ſee why they might not be taught to mend their own ſhoes and ſtockings. Many a brave man, both in the army and navy, is obliged to do theſe things; and, admitting that a married man has a right to require his wife to repair his children's ſtockings, it cannot be expected that ſhe ſhould mend their ſhoes, for that is undoubtedly a maſculine employment; and the father of a family would find it very comfortable to be able by this means to ſave his children from going barefooted. Theſe employments, in addition to the uſual ones of cleaning their own ſhoes, bruſhing their clothes, doing little offices for their maſter, cultivating a garden, &c. if there be one belonging to the ſchool, added to aſſiduous attention to their taſks, would ſufficiently fill up time, and accuſtom youth to induſtry, which might eaſily be directed afterwards to other purſuits.

rity Schools in London. They ſhould alſo by turns do all the houſehold work belonging to the ſchool. Plain work is ſo evidently uſeful to women in general, but to the poor in particular, that no *Charity Girl* can be deemed properly educated who has not attained to a tolerable proficiency at her needle; and there cannot be a want of this kind of work in *Charity Schools* which are upon a ſmall ſcale, if each girl be required not only to ſpin her own clothing, knit her own ſtockings, and make and mend her own clothes; but alſo be allowed to work occaſionally for other branches of the family, in order to eaſe her mother.—But if a ſufficiency of work be not ſupplied by theſe means, *Charity Girls* might contribute greatly to the comfort and conveniency of a neighbourhood by working for ſuch poor women as are obliged to go conſtantly to daily labour, or who cannot uſe a needle themſelves.—It would be a great addition to the comforts of the indigent and neceſſitous if ladies would kindly furniſh materials, either old or new, to be made by Charity Girls into baby linen, or other articles of apparel, for them. Occupations of this kind, under the direction of a clever

clever miſtreſs, would produce reciprocal benefits to thoſe who work and thoſe who receive the fruits of their labour, for by theſe means girls would be trained up not only in habits of induſtry, but of contrivance and economy.

A great part of the buſineſs of religious inſtruction might be carried on while girls were thus occupied at their needles, if the miſtreſſes would read to them, and queſtion them; and if the generality of them learnt to write a tolerable hand, and to do common ſums in the four firſt rules of arithmetic, it would be quite ſufficient.

In *Schools of Induſtry* the buſineſs of literary inſtruction may be contracted into a narrower compaſs. In the ſchool in the pariſh of St. Mary-le-bone before referred to, (ſee page 13) children, both boys and girls, attend the ſchool-rooms and working-rooms alternately. As this inſtitution is upon a very extenſive ſcale, and already includes between 2 and 300 children, it is abſolutely neceſſary to have recourſe to manufactures for employment, for the teachers could not find time to attend to ſo many children employed in the ways I have recommended for *Charity Schools.*—The boys here put heads upon pins, and cloſe ſhoes and boots intended for exportation. The girls ſpin wool for a blanket manufacture, make ſhirts, &c. for a warehouſe, ſpin flax for their own wear, and knit their own ſtockings. They are all taught to read, and ſome of them to write ſufficiently for the common purpoſes of life.

It has been calculated, that ſuppoſing England and Wales to contain ten thouſand pariſhes, and that but ten perſons in every pariſh, one with another, were by ſome method employed who were idle before, then the whole number of perſons ſet to work would be one hundred thouſand; and, if they work but 300 days in a year, and one with another earned but a halfpenny a day, the produce of their labour would at the year's end amount to 62,500 pounds*."—Surely this calculation is a moſt powerful recommendation of Schools of Induſtry; and Mr. Simon's pamphlet, before referred to, furniſhes an unanſwerable argument for the addition of a little *learning*, in the account he has there given of the extreme ignorance of the male felons in the ſix jails of London, Southwark, and Weſtminſter, taken May 11th, 1792.

* See the Propoſal made by the Society for Promoting Chriſtian Knowledge to the Truſtees of Charity Schools, in their annual report, for adding work to learning.

Conſidering

Confidering the extent and variety of the manufactures of this country, one might fuppofe it would not be very difficult to procure employment for boys in Parochial Schools of Induftry; and there is at this time an opening for the employment of many girls in wool-fpinning, for a number of hands have forfaken this occupation to fpin for cotton works, the latter being moft profitable to them. Children in a fchool can fpin for a lower price than thofe perfons who have families to maintain.

I fhall here refer my readers to a Pamphlet written by the Reverend Mr. Bowyer, concerning the rife and progrefs of a fociety for the promotion of induftry in the county of Lincoln*; "the funds of which arife from three fources, *viz.* annual fubfcriptions, limited to *five fhillings* each; cafual benefactions; and parochial fubfcriptions, limited to the proportion of *one per cent.* on the laft year's rate."

"Upon taking a general average of the profits of work done in the different fchools under the direction of this Society, it is clearly

* Sold in London by Meffrs. Harrifon and Co. Bookfellers, in Paternofter Row.

proved

proved that 135 children between 11 and 12 years of age, in the courſe of ten months, taken in the depth of the five preceding winters, earned the ſum of 68ol. 3s. 3d. or half a crown a week each. This is excluſive of all the work done in the other months of thoſe years, excluſive of the work of ſuch ſpinners as were not expert enough to become candidates for certain prizes allotted for the reward of induſtry, and excluſive of work done in other pariſhes for which the ſpinners could claim nothing farther than the price of their labour."

This inſtitution has been conducted with ſuch extraordinary ſucceſs, that a manufacture for ſtuffs of a very fine texture is now completely carried on in a county where, a few years ago, the children in general were totally abandoned to idleneſs.

The annual balls which have been given, firſt at Alford, and afterwards at Lincoln, in which the ladies appeared dreſſed in the ſtuff manufacture of the county, have been of ſingular ſervice to the undertaking. Some lady of high rank is uſually the patroneſs of theſe annual balls; and ſurely thoſe who will thus condeſcend to appear in the fleecy attire

tire of the humble cottager for the purposes of charity, might easily be prevailed upon to contribute towards the establishment of institutions of a similar nature in the vicinity of their Town residences.

I cannot quit the subject of Schools of Industry without speaking of one which is conducted with great success in a retired village, without the aid of any manufacture whatever. This useful establishment is situated at Hartingfordbury, in the county of Hertford *, and took its rise from a Sunday School in that place.

The plan is this:—As the overplus of the Sunday School subscription was not enough to support a School of Industry, the parents of the children willingly agreed to pay three pence *per* week for each scholar. A small sum of money from the Sunday School fund was then laid out in purchasing materials for various articles of clothing at the wholesale prices.

* An account of this school is given in a publication written by the ingenious projector of the plan; the title of it is, "Instructions for cutting out Apparel for the Poor, &c." With a preface, containing a plan for assisting the parents of poor children belonging to Sunday Schools, to clothe them, and other observations. It was originally sold by Mr. Walter, Charing Cross.

prices. Theſe materials were made up in the ſchools into clothing, which was afterwards purchaſed by the parents, allowing them a deduction of one-fourth part of the prime coſt of each article. The apparel purchaſed by the parents in one year was as follows:

36 Aprons, 49 caps, 11 gowns, 19 handkerchiefs, 9 petticoats, 44 ſhifts, 39 ſhirts, 48 pairs of ſtockings, 6 tippets, 69 pairs of ſhoes, 2 ſuits of boys' clothes. The total coſt of this clothing was 33l. 13s. 7d½. It was ſold for 25l. 5s. 2d¾. The expence to the charity was 8l. 4s. 8d½.

In this ſchool, as I have been informed, the girls are employed alternately, one week in knitting, one week in making new apparel, and the third week in mending their own clothes, or thoſe of the family:—they are alſo taught to cut out and contrive the things they make.

Having in a former publication* given my ſentiments reſpecting *Sunday Schools*, I ſhall only ſay at preſent, that repeated experience

* Entitled the Economy of Charity.

perience has fully confirmed my opinion of their efficacy. I ſhall now proceed to make ſome further obſervations upon the *religious inſtruction* given in *Charity Schools.*

Notwithſtanding the plan is ſtill in force which was originally concerted for the purpoſe of giving the children* educated by charity a comprehenſive knowledge of the principles of Chriſtianity, and to exerciſe them betimes in the practice of piety; it muſt be acknowledged, that the education of children brought up in *Charity Schools* is in general very defective in theſe particulars. In order to diſcover from what cauſe the imperfection proceeds, it will be proper to inquire what is now the general mode of putting this plan in execution—which I conceive to be this:

The children, in moſt Charity Schools, are at firſt taught to read in a Spelling Book, the leſſons of which conſiſt chiefly of ſentences collected from the ſcriptures, moſt of them in figurative language; as ſoon as they can read and ſpell a little, they are put into the New Teſtament, and when they have read this from beginning to end, they proceed to the

* See Page 17.

Old Teſtament, and go through that in the ſame manner, without regard to any thing farther than improvement in the *art of reading*. They learn, by ſtated regular taſks, the columns of ſpelling in the Spelling Book; and in ſome ſchools they are taught Engliſh grammar, writing, and arithmetic. Once or twice a week the ſcholars are catechiſed, that is, they ſtand up in claſſes, and anſwer in rotation the queſtions in the Church Catechiſm, and explanations of it. They learn, perhaps, beſides, chapters, prayers, &c. by heart, and are ſometimes taught pſalmody. They go to church twice every Sunday, and, where there is weekly duty performed, they attend alſo on Wedneſdays, Fridays, and Holidays. When the ſcholars leave ſchool to go out into the world as ſervants or apprentices, a Bible, Common Prayer Book, and Whole Duty of Man, are given to them; and it is ſuppoſed, from the years they have been at ſchool, they muſt neceſſarily be furniſhed with a competent ſhare of Chriſtian knowledge to enable them to read with advantage and improvement as long as they live.

How far the original plan of education anſwered

ſwered at the firſt introduction of Charity Schools, is not eaſy to determine at this diſtance of time; but, for ſeveral obvious reaſons, we may ſuppoſe that it was more effectual then than it is now; for it was very natural for thoſe whoſe zeal for the reformed religion led them to eſtabliſh and endow theſe ſchools, to continue their zeal towards the objects of their benevolence, to give perſonal attendance, and to examine the children themſelves, in order to ſee whether their deſign was properly executed. Add to this, that public catechiſing was much more generally practiſed in former times than it has been of late years, as a means of preſerving the principles of orthodox Chriſtianity from corruption. So that, moſt probably, the children who were firſt received into Charity Schools had the benefit of more *verbal inſtruction* than thoſe who now fill their places: of courſe they were not left, as many of the latter are, to the diſcretion of teachers ill qualified to explain difficult words and phraſes, and illuſtrate points of doctrine, which frequently require to be placed in a variety of lights to be accommodated to the comprehenſion of children.

How

How the laudable cuſtom of catechiſing fell into ſuch diſuſe, I will not take upon me to ſay. It has been imputed to the unwillingneſs of the poor to ſend their children to be catechiſed; but ſurely this cannot be juſtly urged againſt the teachers in Charity Schools, who ought not to have a matter of ſuch moment left to their option.

In many pariſhes the good old cuſtoms above mentioned are ſtill kept up through the piety and benevolence of the reſident miniſters and other truſtees, and a very manifeſt difference is obſervable between the children educated under theſe advantages, and thoſe who have them not; yet I hope I may be allowed to ſay, without giving offence, that there is room for improvement upon the original plan, even when conducted with the greateſt zeal and attention; and that where theſe are wanting, and the teacher is deficient in knowledge or judgment, whatever means can be deviſed to ſupply the deficiency of *verbal inſtruction*, have a reaſonable claim to the conſideration of the patrons of the poor, and the friends of Chriſtianity, who cannot be inſenſible of the dangers to which the riſing generation is expoſed expofed in this age of controverfy and infidelity.

I would by no means wifh to make the children of the poor *cafuifts* in religion; but it furely is defirable that they fhould have as extenfive an acquaintance with its principles as they have leifure for acquiring; and of this thofe who are put to Charity Schools have a confiderable portion, few of them having much manual employment.

Time is too valuable to be wafted or mifapplied, yet it is an undeniable fact that there is a confiderable lofs of time and mifapplication of ftudy in many of the *Charity Schools* which are liberally endowed, and where the courfe of inftruction is profeffedly very comprehenfive, as any one may convince himfelf by examining the children belonging to them. I am forry to reckon in the portion of ill-fpent time that which is paffed by many in the houfe of God, but thofe who occafionally attend on week days fome of the churches, both in town and country, of which Charity Children form almoft the whole of the congregation, have indifputable proofs, from the irreverent behaviour of the boys and girls when the eye of the mafter or miftrefs is not watching over them, and the manner in which they make the reſponſes, that they neither conſider where they are, or what they go to church for; and yet it is more than probable, that theſe very children can repeat many paſſages of Scripture by heart, as well as the anſwers of the church catechiſm, and explanations of it, &c.

In making theſe remarks, I do not mean to impute *careleſſneſs* or *neglect* to the teachers; it is very likely they have done their duty to the beſt of their abilities: their ſcholars can read, write, and caſt accounts, and have learnt every thing uſually taught to Charity Children; we muſt therefore ſeek another cauſe to which the deficiencies here pointed out are aſſignable.—I do not ſcruple to ſay that they are in a great meaſure to be aſcribed to the prevailing method of exercising the memories of children in learning by rote leſſons greatly above their capacities, and ſuffaring them to read without reflection, inhead of ihitiating them by ſuch ſimple inſtructions as would gradually unfold their underſtandings, and render their minds capable of receiving laſting impreſſions concerning things of the utmoſt importance to their preſent and future happineſs.

The generality of *religious books*, now uſed

in *Charity Schools*, have been written by men of deep erudition. Such authors, accuſtomed to read the works of the learned, and to compoſe in elegant language themſelves, are apt to conclude that what is familiar to their own cultivated underſtandings muſt be univerſally intelligible; but it is far otherwiſe—the totally illiterate require previous inſtruction to prepare their minds for thoſe leſſons, which, however good and excellent, are almoſt as obſcure to them as if they were written in a dead language.

It requires perſonal experience in the employment of teaching children of the lower claſſes of life, to enable any perſon to form an accurate judgment in reſpect to what they are capable of underſtanding: of this experience I have had a conſiderable ſhare, having for ſeveral years given regular attendance as a viſiter in Sunday Schools; I have alſo had frequent opportunities of examining children brought up in Charity Schools, and am convinced that the latter, in general, do little more than ſtore their memories with *words* and *ſentences*, or at beſt obtain a few crude indiſtinct notions of the great truths of

Chriſtianity, unleſs they are ſo fortunate as to have very intelligent teachers to aſſiſt them in their ſtudies by *verbal inſtructions*, ſuited to their tender capacities; the number of whom is proportionably very ſmall, though ſufficient to prove, by compariſon, that the books in general uſe in *Charity Schools* are not fully adequate to the end of conveying to young minds ſuch a thorough knowledge of the principles of religion as children ought to acquire in theſe ſchools, conſidering the time which is apparently devoted to the attainment of it.

I would not be ſuſpected of entertaining a wiſh to ſee the valuable and condeſcending labours of ſome of the firſt writers laid entirely aſide to make way for compoſitions unworthy of being compared with them. No! far humbler are my views; I only deſire to ſee the works of the learned rendered effectual by means of books, in a more ſimple ſtile, which may gradually lead on to them. Of ſuch books my propoſed publications for the children of the poor will conſiſt; and I am much miſtaken, if the others will not be ſought with more earneſtneſs, and beſtowed to more advantage, after the minds of the

ſcholars

ſcholars have been prepared for comprehending their important contents.

The project of forming a practical ſyſtem of education for the children of the poor has been long in my thoughts, and this is the ſecond effort I have made towards the accompliſhment of it.—The firſt conſiſted of the *Sunday School Catechiſt*, and *Sunday Scholar's Manual*; in which I attempted to prove, in a familiar manner, "The certainty of Divine Revelation—The truth and authenticity of the Scriptures—To give exalted ideas of the perfections of the ſupreme Being; and to fill up the outline of religious and moral duties, drawn with a moſt maſterly hand in that part of the Church Catechiſm which relates to our duty to God, and our duty to our neighbour."

The works now offered to the world are not deſigned as a *ſequel* to thoſe I here refer to, but as conſtituent parts of the propoſed plan of appropriate inſtruction for the poor, which begins with the firſt rudiments of ſchool tuition, and proceeds gradually to inſtructions ſuited to ſcholars in the higheſt claſſes, previouſly to their entrance into active life. In this ſyſtem the above books will be introduced, together with others of various authors.

The articles which I purpose to furnish towards this course of appropriate instruction are the following:

I. A Spelling Book calculated for Charity Schools, in two Parts.—Part I. Containing the Alphabet—Easy Lessons—and Stories of Boys and Girls, in words of one syllable only. Part II. Consisting of Words divided into Syllables—Easy Lessons—Instructive Fables—Lessons with Scripture Names to prepare the scholar for reading the Bible with fluency, &c.

II. Scripture Lessons, extracted from the historical books of the Old Testament.

III. Scripture Lessons from the New Testament.

IV. Moral Instructions, collected from the Scriptures, suited to the practice of children and youth, to be committed to memory.

V. Lessons on the Liturgy, &c. in the Book of Common Prayer.

VI. Exemplary Tales, calculated to promote the practice of religion and virtue in the various occupations of humble life.

VII. The Teacher's Assistant, containing full

full directions for teaching, lecturing, and examining the children from day to day, as they proceed through the foregoing books.

The Spelling Book, the Abridgment of Scripture Hiftory, and two fmall volumes of the Teacher's Affiftant, are already publifhed.

The following reafons, added to the obfervations already made upon the books ufed in Charity Schools, will, I truft, be admitted as a fufficient apology for the undertaking.

I am very fenfible that there is already a great variety of *Spelling Books*, by means of which hundreds of children have been taught to read and fpell fuccefsfully; but I do not know of one to which I could have adapted the inftruction which it was my defign to give in the *Teacher's Affiftant:* this difficulty induced me to compofe a Spelling Book myfelf.

There is one article of it in particular which I have not met with in other Spelling Books—*Leffons* with *Scripture Names*, intended to prepare the children for reading the Bible with fluency.

In refpect to the Abridgment of the Old and New Teftament, to be ufed by learners inftead of the Bible itfelf, I fubmit it to the judgment of the moſt experienced inſtructors, whether children gain a competent knowledge, even of *Scripture Hiſtory*, much leſs of the *Principles of Chriſtianity*, by reading the entire contents of the ſacred writings without diſcrimination? And whether ſuch a method be not more likely to give them a diſtaſte for the Scriptures, than to excite in their minds a deſire to read and ſtudy them to the end of their lives?

The *Scriptures*, among other particulars which diſtinguiſh them from all the compoſitions of human art, and prove their divine original, have this remarkable one—that they are written to ſuit all ranks of people in the ſucceſſive ages of the world, and every individual of them in all the various circumſtances of human life; conſequently the *whole* of the ſacred writings cannot be deſigned by the great Author of them for the particular ſtudy of every perſon in every period of life, and in the various conditions or circumſtances in which each may, in the courſe of this earthly exiſtence, be placed.

The Bible is a moſt comprehenſive volume, and thoſe perſons whoſe faculties have been enlarged by the moſt liberal education, and

and who have full leiſure to ſtudy its multifarious contents, find numberleſs texts, and frequently whole paſſages, wrapped in impenetrable obſcurity, from the cauſe above alluded to; that they were peculiarly adapted to the circumſtances of generations that have paſſed away, or of generations yet to come. Various parts of ſcripture relating to the Jewiſh conſtitution, are inſtances of the former; and among the latter may be reckoned ſuch prophecies as remain yet to be fulfilled.

The great object in reading the inſpired writings certainly ought to be, to derive ſpiritual improvement from them; but can this be done to good effect by ignorant children reading it in the uſual way, either by themſelves or in a claſs? On the contrary, is it not a kind of profanation of the *word of God*, to make the ſacred volume a mere *teaching book*, over which learners are to ſtammer and blunder to no good purpoſe? for children cannot eaſily learn by this practice, even to read with fluency and propriety, much leſs to reflect on the power, wiſdom, and goodneſs of God in the works of creation, redemption, and providence. That it was the deſign of the Creator and Governor of the world, that children ſhould

have

have an early acquaintance with his word, we may learn from the ſcriptures themſelves. *The words which God has commanded you,* ſaid Moſes to the Iſraelites, *ye ſhall lay up in your hearts; and ye ſhall teach them diligently unto your children**. *Train up a child in the way he ſhould go*, ſaid the wiſeſt of men, *and when he is old he will not depart from it*†; and the prophet Iſaiah ſays, *Whom ſhall he* (the LORD) *teach knowledge? And whom ſhall he make to underſtand doctrine? Them that are weaned from the milk, and drawn from the breaſts*‡.

But the ſame prophet adds, *Precept muſt be upon precept, and line upon line; here a little and there a little*; which plainly points out to us that religious knowledge ſhould be communicated to the young and ignorant by *degrees*. How juſtly would that teacher be condemned who ſhould ſet his pupil to read Euclid's Elements before he knew even the firſt rule in arithmetic; and is it not equally unreaſonable to require children to go through the Scriptures, beginning with the New Teſtament too, before they know the firſt principles of religion?

* Deut. vi. 6. † Prov. xxvi. 6. ‡ Iſai. xxviii. 9, 10.

To effect this something appears to me to be wanting in a more *familiar stile* than the excellent directions for a devout and decent behaviour at public worship, which are usually bound up with the Common Prayer Books, supplied to Charity Schools by the Society for the Propagation of Christian knowledge: something that will awaken attention to every sentence of the service.

The end proposed by the Moral Tales which I purpose to furnish is to give the scholars a taste for improving books, and a contempt for those pernicious publications by which they very often corrupt their minds.

It now only remains to give some account of the *Teacher's Assistant.* The first volume of this work corresponds with the first part of the *Charity School Spelling Book.* It begins with instructions concerning the alphabet, and explains the lessons as the children read them. To these instructions are added lectures interspersed with questions. Some of these Lectures (being adapted to a Day School of Industry) are designed to make the scholars sensible of the blessing of a good education, the obligation they lay themselves under when they gain admittance into a school supported

ſupported by charity, to keep punctually to the rules of it; the gratitude they owe to their benefactors; and the advantages of induſtry.—The ſubſequent Lectures are intended for the uſe of Charity Schools of all denominations, being upon the firſt principles of Religion.

The ſecond volume contains inſtructions ſuited to Part II. of the Charity School Spelling Book. The Leſſons with Scripture names are divided and accented, that the Teacher may be at no loſs in reſpect to dividing or pronouncing them. Theſe inſtructions are followed by another ſet of Lectures, interſperſed with Queſtions, upon the Divine Plan of Redemption; by means of which the ſcholars are conducted on a ſtep farther in Religious Knowledge. To theſe Lectures is added an explanation of the Prayers and Hymns at the end of the Spelling Book. It is my intention to extend the *Teacher's Aſſiſtant* till it comprehends an explanation of every leſſon which the ſcholars read or learn by heart, in the books prepared for their uſe. When the ſcholars ſhall have gone through the above books with the correſponding Lectures, I hope they will be able to ſearch the

Scriptures

Scriptures themſelves, to underſtand Sermons, explanations of the Catechiſm, &c. and to improve their minds by reading the many excellent books which have been written for their edification, in a ſuperior ſtile, by the learned.

I have not a doubt but that in general all poſſible care is taken by the truſtees of Charity Schools in the choice of teachers, but though ſome few of the latter have had a proper education, the majority of them are incapable of giving verbal inſtructions on religious ſubjects. It is true that a moſt excellent plan has been laid down for them in Dr. Talbot's *Chriſtian Schoolmaſter*, but very few are competent to the execution of it. In the *Teacher's Aſſiſtant* I aſpire to the honour of co-operating with the pious author of this moſt judicious and uſeful work, which I ſhall make uſe of as a direction to myſelf. My principal aim is to put maſters and miſtreſſes of Charity Schools into a method of giving that moral and religious inſtruction which the reverend author adviſes.

Nor will the courſe of inſtruction here propoſed appear too extenſive, I truſt, if it be conſidered that the greateſt part of it is given in the

the ſtile of familiar converſation, and will not occupy ſo much of the children's time as a more contracted courſe, in which they are required to commit to memory the words of the explanations of the Catechiſm, Common Prayer, &c. It is certainly proper they ſhould have ſome taſks of this nature; but let me add, there are beſides *memory* other faculties in the mind, of even the meaneſt human creature, which require culture.

Children admitted into Charity Schools have uſually ſeveral years tuition.—What a happy opportunity does this afford for imparting to them a perfect knowledge of the principles of Chriſtianity! Surely *theſe* children at leaſt may be taught every part of that holy religion which was deſigned by the divine Author of it for the Poor as well as the Rich.—There is no occaſion to confine *them* to what are uſually called the *moral parts* of the ſcripture; neither is it in fact neceſſary to circumſcribe thoſe educated in *Schools of Induſtry* and *Sunday Schools* within ſuch narrow bounds.

*Faith* is a general concern as well as *morality*, for it is as plainly required in the New Teſtament. Our bleſſed Lord called upon all kinds of people *to have faith*, which he would

not

not have done, if he had not known that all might have it who were willing to believe the revealed word of God. So far fiom defiring that the myfteries of the gofpel revelation fhould be withheld from the lower orders of people, our Saviour vouchfafed to inftruct multitudes of them himfelf in the moft fublime truths of his holy religion.—He told them without referve, that he was the Son of God; that he was one with the Father; that he fhould lay down his life for mankind; that there is a Holy Ghoft, who is alfo one with the Father and the Son; and many other particulars: and he exprefsly enjoined his apoftles *to preach the gofpel to the poor*.—He alfo faid to his difciples, *Suffer little children to come unto me, and forbid them not*;—and one of his laft injunctions to Peter was, *Feed my lambs.* All this the Apoftles did—*freely they had received*, and *freely they gave*; not with a niggardly hand did they difpenfe the bread of life, but with unbounded liberality;—the Spirit of God co-operated with them, and the word multiplied like the loaves and fifhes.—From hence we may fully infer that the poor, in all fucceeding ages, ought to be made acquainted, not merely with fuch parts of fcripture as relate to *moral duties*, but with thofe alfo which relate to *Chriftian Faith*; and childhood is the proper feafon for receiving the rudiments of religious knowledge, as well as of other learning.

I will venture to affert, from my own experience, that it is as practicable to teach children every point of Chriftian doctrine, as the plaineft moral precept in either the Old or New Teftament.—The prefent ftate of religion in this country calls loudly for the experiment; and where can it be made with more propriety than in Charity Schools? which were at firft eftablifhed for the exprefs purpofe of training the poor in the genuine principles of the reformed religion.—If in former times it was thought neceffary to guard the rifing generation againft the *errors of popery*, it is equally fo now to fortify young minds againft falfe opinions of as fatal a tendency. In order to enforce what I have here afferted concerning Chriftian Faith, I fhall take the liberty of borrowing fome of the powerful arguments of a learned prelate*, which, though addreffed to the clergy of a particular diocefe, are of general application.

To pretend that " faith and practice are fe-

* See the prefent Bifhop of St. David's Charge to the Clergy of his Diocefe in the year 1790.

parable

parable things (ſays the learned and pious author) is a groſs miſtake, or rather a manifeſt contradiction—practical holineſs is the end; faith is the means; and to ſuppoſe faith and practice ſeparable, is to ſuppoſe the end attainable without the uſe of the means. The direct contrary is the truth. The practice of religion will always thrive, in proportion as its doctrines are generally underſtood and firmly received; and the practice will degenerate and decay, in proportion as the doctrine is miſunderſtood and neglected.

"I am well aware, that it has been very much the faſhion to ſuppoſe a great want of capacity in the common people, to be carried any great length in religious knowledge, more than in the abſtruſe ſciences. That the world and all things in it had a Maker; that the Maker of the world made man, and gave him the life which he now enjoys; that he who firſt gave life, can at any time reſtore it; that he can puniſh in a future life, crimes which he ſuffers to be committed with impunity in this; ſome of theſe firſt principles of religion the vulgar, it is ſuppoſed, may be brought to comprehend. But the peculiar doctrines of revelation, the Trinity of perſons in the undivided

 Godhead,

Godhead, the incarnation of the ſecond perſon, the expiation of ſin by the Redeemer's ſufferings, the efficacy of his interceſſion, the myſterious commerce of the believer's ſoul with the divine Spirit—theſe things are ſuppoſed to be far above their reach.

"If this were really the caſe, the condition of mankind would indeed be miſerable, and the proffer of mercy in the goſpel little better than a mockery of their woe. For the conſequence would be, that the common people could never be carried beyond the firſt principles of what is called natural religion. Of the efficacy of Natural Religion as a rule of action, the world has had the long experience of 1600 years; for ſo much was the interval between the inſtitution of the Moſaic church and the publication of the Goſpel. During that interval certainly, if not from an earlier period, Natural Religion was left to try its powers on the heathen world. The reſult of the experiment is, that its powers are of no avail. Among the vulgar, Natural Religion never produced any effect at all; among the learned much of it is to be found in their writings, little in their lives. But if this Natural Religion, a thing of no practical efficacy, as experiment

periment has demonſtrated, be the utmoſt of religion which the common people can receive; then is our preaching vain, Chriſt died in vain, and man muſt periſh. Bleſſed be God, the caſe is far otherwiſe. As we have on the one ſide experimental proof of the inſignificance of what is called Natural Religion; ſo on the other, in the ſucceſs of the firſt preachers of Chriſtianity, we have an experimental proof of the ſufficiency of Revealed Religion to thoſe very ends, in which Natural Religion failed. In their ſucceſs we have experimental proof, that there is nothing in the great myſtery of godlineſs, which the vulgar, more than the learned, want capacity to apprehend; ſince upon the firſt preaching of the Goſpel, the illiterate, the ſcorn of phariſaical pride, who knew not the law, and were therefore deemed accurſed, were the firſt to underſtand, and to embrace the Chriſtian Doctrine.

" Nor will this ſeem ſtrange, if it be conſidered, that Religion and Science are very different things, and the objects of different faculties. Science is the object of natural Reaſon; Religious Truth, of Faith. Faith, like the natural faculties, may be improved by exerciſe; but in its beginning it is unqueſtionably

ably a diſtinct gift of God. Were it otherwiſe the common people would be juſt as incapable of receiving theſe principles of natural religion, which are thought ſo ſimple, and ſo much within the reach of popular apprehenſion, as the higher myſteries of the Goſpel; for I ſcruple not to aſſert, that no proof can be more ſubtle in its proceſs, or in its principles more abſtruſe, however juſt in its concluſions, than the arguments which philoſophy furniſhes, of the being and attributes of God, and the immortality of the human ſoul. By mere argument, therefore, addreſſed to their reaſon, no conviction could be wrought, in the minds of the common people, of the very firſt principles of Religion. By Faith, their minds are opened to apprehend all that is revealed of the ſcheme of Redemption, no leſs than the very firſt principles, the doctrine of a reſurrection, or the firſt creation of the world out of nothing.—A want of capacity in theſe ſubjects, is a want of Faith; and the ſurmiſe of the want of Faith in the common people, more than in their betters, is in truth a diſtruſt of God; as if he ſhould be wanting to his own work, and fail to give all men Faith to receive a diſcovery, made by

his

his exprefs command, or rather by Himfelf, to all, of a fcheme of mercy in which all are interefted.

—" The notion that religion and morality are the fame, generally as it has too long prevailed, needs no other confutation, but what will fpontaneoufly arife from a juft definition of the terms. Religion in the practical part is a ftudious conformity of our actions, our wills, and our appetites, to the revealed will of God, in pure regard to the divine authority, and to the relation, in which we ftand to God, as difcovered to us by revelation. Morality is a conformity of our actions to the relation in which we ftand to each other in civil fociety. Morality therefore comprehends fome confiderable part, but a part only, of the duties of the fecond table. Morality enjoins filial piety; it prohibits murder, adultery, theft, falfe witnefs, and thofe inferior crimes, which for the like harm that in a lefs degree they bring to fociety, or to the individual in fociety, bear affinity to thofe, as to the heads of fo many different fpecies. But does Morality fay, *Thou fhalt not covet?* Does the control of moral obligation reach the fecret meditations of the mind, and the filent defires of the heart?

heart? Does it impofe reftraint upon the fenfuality of the imagination, and the private prurience of appetite? Like the Divine Law, does it extend to every fecret energy of the mind, the will, and the appetite, and require the obedience of the inner as well as the outer man? Again, doth Morality fay, *Thou fhalt love thine enemies; thou fhalt blefs them that curfe; do good to them that perfecute?* Doth morality enjoin *forgivenefs of injuries, or the giving of alms to the poor?* Truly, morality *careth for none of thefe things.* How fmall a part then of focial duty, of a Chriftian's focial duty, is the utmoft which Morality exacts; and how fatally are they mifled who are taught that mere Morality fatisfies the law by which the Chriftian fhall be judged, even in the inferior branch.

" With the higher branch of duty, with the love of God, and of confequence with the duties of the firft table, Morality hath evidently no concern or connection. The worfhip which I owe to God, is certainly no part of the duty which I owe to man. It is indifferent to Morality, whether I worfhip one God or many. Morality is not offended if I worfhip graven images. Morality enjoins no obſervance of one day in ſeven; no feaſt of faith in ſacramental rites upon the body and blood of the Redeemer. For Reaſon, from which Morality derives her whole authority and information; Reaſon knows not, till ſhe has been taught by the lively oracles of God, that the Creator of the world is the ſole object of worſhip; ſhe knows of no prohibition of particular modes of worſhip; ſhe knows nothing of the creation of the world in ſeven days; nothing of redemption; nothing of the ſpiritual life, and the food brought down from Heaven for its ſuſtenance. Morality, therefore, having no better inſtructreſs than this ignorant Reaſon, hath no ſenſe or knowledge of any part of that great branch of duty which comes under the general title of devotion. Let me conjure you therefore, my brethren, to be cautious how you admit, much more how you propagate, that deluſive dangerous maxim, that *morality is the ſum of practical religion*, leſt you place the totality and perfection of the thing in a very inconſiderable part."—So far the learned Prelate.

I ſhall not preſume to add a word more upon the ſubject of religious inſtruction; the application of the excellent reaſoning here

 produced,

produced, is ſufficiently obvious. Teachers of Charity Schools are the immediate ſubordinates of the clergy; and it is their indiſpenſable duty to prepare their ſcholars for the examination of their reſpective miniſters. The generality profeſs and attempt to do ſo, but with how little ſucceſs I have endeavoured to ſhew, not with a view to injure, but to ſerve and aſſiſt them.—May the bleſſing of the Almighty attend the labours of all who unite in ſo important a cauſe as that of ſpreading the knowledge of Chriſtianity among the Poor!

THE END.

For EU product safety concerns, contact us at Calle de José Abascal, 56–1°, 28003 Madrid, Spain or eugpsr@cambridge.org.

www.ingramcontent.com/pod-product-compliance
Ingram Content Group UK Ltd.
Pitfield, Milton Keynes, MK11 3LW, UK
UKHW012336130625
459647UK00009B/311

* 9 7 8 1 1 0 8 0 1 8 8 6 9 *